Beyond Auto

Cooperative Human-Machine Development

Taylor Royce

DEDICATION

To all developers who strive to be the best and be innovative, thank you. Your continuous pursuit of excellence and ardor for technology inspire all of us. This book is dedicated to helping you continue to grow and be productive. Keep shaping the future, pushing limits, and tearing down obstacles. To your next journey into coding, cheers!

CONTENTS

ACKNOWLEDGMENTS

I am truly grateful to everyone who helped to make this book, "Beyond Automation: Cooperative Human-Machine Development," possible.

I want to start by expressing my gratitude to my family and friends for their consistent support and motivation along this journey. I've found motivation and stability in your belief in me.

I owe a debt of gratitude to all the developers, engineers, and business leaders whose knowledge and perspectives have enhanced the information in this book. It is very admirable how committed you are to sharing knowledge and developing technologies.

I owe a debt of thanks to the many authors, bloggers, and instructors whose work on the topic of cooperative human-machine development has influenced and informed me.

I would especially like to express my gratitude to the active online forums and groups, where interesting conversations and shared experiences have helped me better comprehend this intricate topic.

Finally, I would like to thank each and every one of you who has read this book. Your curiosity about the nexus between technology and humanity inspires me to keep researching and promoting cooperative strategies that spur advancement.

I'd like to thank everyone for joining me on this rewarding trip.

DISCLAIMER

This book, "Beyond Automation: Cooperative Human-Machine Development," contains content that is just meant to be informative. Despite having taken every precaution to guarantee the content's accuracy and completeness, the author disclaims all express and implied representations and guarantees on the availability, suitability, accuracy, completeness, and reliability of the material provided here.

You consequently absolutely assume all risk associated with any reliance you may have on such material. The author disclaims all responsibility for any loss or harm, including but not limited to indirect or consequential loss or damage, or any other kind of loss or damage resulting from lost profits or data resulting from using this book.

Any links, references, or advice included here does not always imply endorsement of the ideas or recommendations contained within.

Every attempt has been made to uphold intellectual property

rights and copyrights. In order to address any inadvertent infringements, kindly get in touch with the author directly.

CHAPTER 1

MACHINES TAKE OVER

In the contemporary world, artificial intelligence (AI) is a transformational force that is redefining industries and changing society as a whole.

1.1 A Synopsis of AI's Development from Theory to Practice

The development of artificial intelligence (AI) from a theoretical idea to a useful technology is an amazing tale of technological achievement and human inventiveness.

Alan Turing and the Turing Test (1950)

- **Early Theories and Foundations:** The concept that computers may mimic human intelligence was first presented by Alan Turing, who is frequently regarded as the father of computer science. In his 1950 work "Computing Machinery and Intelligence," Alan Turing established the Turing

Test, which became a cornerstone of artificial intelligence research. It postulated that a machine may be deemed intelligent if it could converse with a human intelligibly.

- **1956 Dartmouth Conference:** The phrase "artificial intelligence" was first used during the Dartmouth Conference, where scientists gathered to talk about how machines could be able to carry out tasks that would normally need human intelligence. This occasion signified the beginning of AI as a separate academic discipline.

Theoretical Advancements and Obstacles

- **Expert Systems and Symbolic AI in the 1960s and 1980s:** Symbolic AI, in which systems were constructed using clear rules and logic, was the main emphasis of early AI research. Expert systems gained popularity as they imitated human decision-making in particular fields by using knowledge bases. But because of these systems' shortcomings and the lack of financing, there were "AI winters," or periods of disillusionment.

- **The Revival of Neural Networks in the 1980s and**

1990s: Advances in neural networks, which were motivated by the composition and operation of the human brain, reignited interest in artificial intelligence. The discovery of backpropagation algorithms in the 1980s made neural network training more efficient, despite early difficulties.

Evolution of Machine Learning in the Modern Era

- **Big Data and Computational Power (2000s–present):** AI is back, thanks to the growth of data and increases in computing power. Large datasets and potent hardware are used by machine learning (ML) and deep learning (DL), two emerging concepts, to produce astounding outcomes.

- **Innovations and Practical Applications**: From defeating human champions in challenging games like Go to enabling self-driving automobiles, modern AI has made enormous strides. Artificial intelligence (AI) has become a core component of many applications, such as robots, computer vision, and natural language processing (NLP).

1.2 Demystifying AI: Automation, Deep Learning, and Machine Learning

Gaining an understanding of AI's fundamental elements is necessary to appreciate both its strengths and weaknesses.

Machine Learning (ML)

Definition and Approach: Creating algorithms that let computers learn from and forecast data is the main goal of machine learning, a branch of artificial intelligence. In contrast to traditional programming, which involves explicitly coding rules, machine learning algorithms find patterns and relationships in the data.

Types of Machine Learning

1. **Supervised learning:** Training models using labeled data with known desired output is known as supervised learning. Predictive analytics, spam detection, and image categorization are some examples of applications.

2. **Unsupervised Learning:** works with unlabeled data and looks for structures or patterns that are concealed. Anomaly detection and clustering are two

examples.

3. **Reinforcement Learning:** Uses rewards for desired behaviors to teach agents how to make decisions. It is extensively utilized in autonomous systems, gaming, and robotics.

Neural Networks and Hierarchical Learning
Deep Learning (DL):

A kind of machine learning called deep learning uses multi-layered artificial neural networks, or deep neural networks, to simulate intricate patterns. With the help of each layer's extraction of higher-level information from the raw input, the system is able to accurately perform tasks like voice and image recognition.

New Architectures:

- **Neural Nets with Convolution (CNNs):** CNNs have completely changed computer vision applications; they are mostly utilized for image and video processing.

- **RNNs (Recurrent Neural Networks):** RNNs are useful for jobs like language modeling and time-series forecasting because they are made for sequential data. Traditional RNN problems are addressed by Long Short-Term Memory (LSTM) and Gated Recurrent Units (GRUs), which improve long-term dependency handling.

Robotic Process Automation (RPA):

- **Automation** RPA is the process of automating rule-based, repetitive processes that humans normally undertake by using software robots. It is extensively utilized in company operations like customer support, invoicing processing, and data entering.

- **AI-Driven Automation:** handles more complicated and dynamic activities by fusing standard automation methods with AI technology. Intelligent virtual assistants, smart manufacturing, and driverless cars are a few examples.

1.3 The Effect on Industries: Healthcare and Manufacturing

AI is influencing many different industries and promoting efficiency and innovation.

Production

- **Intelligent Manufacturing and Industry 4.0:** Smart factories, where robots interact and cooperate with minimal human intervention, are made possible by IoT devices and AI-powered automation. Key applications include supply chain optimization, quality control, and predictive maintenance.

- **Automation and Robotics:** AI-driven advanced robotics improve productivity and accuracy in manufacturing processes. Cobots, or collaborative robots, assist humans in their work by enhancing their abilities and guaranteeing their security.

Medicine

- **Findings and Therapy:** Artificial intelligence (AI) systems examine medical pictures, including MRIs and X-rays, to help make highly accurate diagnoses. Predictive analytics is used to create individualized treatment strategies that enhance patient outcomes.

- **Drug Discovery and Development:** AI finds and predicts the efficacy of prospective drug candidates by evaluating large datasets, which speeds up the process of finding new drugs. This shortens the time and expense involved in introducing novel medications to the market.

- **Virtual Health Assistants:** AI-powered chatbots and virtual assistants improve patient access to healthcare services by giving patients information, making appointments, and providing initial diagnosis.

Money

- **Algorithmic Trading:** AI systems evaluate market data instantly, placing transactions at the best times to optimize profits. Key applications include quantitative analysis and high-frequency trading.
- **Fraud Detection:** By identifying patterns suggestive of fraudulent activity, machine learning algorithms enable proactive financial crime detection and prevention.
- **consumer Service:** Chatbots and virtual assistants driven by AI improve consumer interactions by offering tailored financial guidance and assistance.

Retail

- **Personalized Shopping Experiences:** AI uses consumer data analysis to provide targeted marketing campaigns and personalized product suggestions that increase customer pleasure and engagement.

- **Inventory Management:** By optimizing inventory levels, predictive analytics lowers the expenses related to stockouts or overstocking.

- **Supply Chain Optimization:** Artificial intelligence (AI) optimizes supply chain and logistics processes, guaranteeing timely delivery and reducing interruptions.

1.4 The Double-Edged Sword: Job Displacement vs. Efficiency Gains

Even though artificial intelligence has many advantages, there are still issues that need to be resolved.

Efficiency Gains

- **Increased Productivity:** By freeing up human labor to concentrate on higher-value tasks, automation of repetitive jobs increases overall productivity.

- **Cost Savings:** AI-driven optimizations lower operating expenses, increasing a company's profitability.

- **Innovation and Growth:** AI makes it possible to create new goods and services, which spurs economic expansion and innovation.

Automation of Routine Tasks

- **Job Displacement:** There is a significant chance that jobs involving repetitive and rule-based tasks will become automated. Jobs in data entry, manufacturing, and customer service fall under this category.

- **Skill Modifications and Novel Prospects:** AI generates new opportunities needing high technical abilities, but it also displaces some employment. By gaining knowledge in AI, data science, and related subjects, workers must adapt.

- **Contributions to Society and Economy:** Ineffective management of job relocation might result in social unrest and income disparity. To assist impacted workers, governments and organizations need to fund retraining and upskilling initiatives.

Weighting the Trade-Offs

- **Regulation and Policy:** States must create rules that safeguard workers' rights while promoting the proper use of AI. This entails upholding just labor norms and encouraging moral AI practices.

- **Training and Education:** Curriculum must be modified by educational establishments to provide students with the abilities required in an AI-driven future. Programs for lifelong learning should be encouraged in order to assist employees in adjusting to new jobs.

- **Teamwork Initiatives:** For the benefits of artificial intelligence to be widely distributed in a sustainable and inclusive future, businesses, governments, and educational institutions must work together.

The development of AI is a critical juncture in human history that brings both previously unheard-of potential and difficulties. We may successfully traverse the complexity of this technology revolution and realize its promise for the greater good by comprehending its evolution, essential elements, and effects.

CHAPTER 2

The Changing Work Environment

The rapid growth of AI and associated technologies is causing a substantial upheaval in the workplace.

2.1 Cooperative AI and Humans: A Novel Dynamic

AI integration is bringing about a new dynamic in the workplace where humans and robots collaborate to achieve increased productivity and creativity.

Improved Decision-Making

- **Insights Driven by Data:** AI systems are able to process enormous volumes of data at very fast speeds, giving rise to insights that facilitate better decision-making for people. Businesses can more accurately spot trends, predict results, and optimize tactics thanks to this collaboration.
- **Enhanced Perception:** AI enhances human

judgment by making recommendations based on data analysis, not taking the place of it. AI, for instance, can evaluate patient data in the medical field to help physicians diagnose conditions and suggest therapies, improving clinical decision-making.

Productivity and Efficiency

- **Automating Daily Tasks:** Artificial intelligence (AI) is excellent at handling monotonous, repetitive jobs, freeing up human workers to concentrate on more intricate and creative work. AI-powered chatbots handle basic enquiries in fields like finance and customer service, freeing up human workers to handle more complex problems.

- **Improved Cooperation Instruments:** Artificial intelligence (AI)-enabled project management platforms and virtual assistants facilitate teamwork by streamlining processes and enhancing communication. These tools support easy information sharing, work prioritization, and scheduling management.

Creative AI Applications

- **Innovation and Creativity:** Artificial intelligence (AI) is being employed in creative industries like music, design, and art, where it works in tandem with human creators to produce original ideas and thoughts. AI algorithms, for example, can help with product design, music composition, and even literary writing.

- **Innovation and Co-Creation:** The combination between human creativity and machine intelligence produces creative ideas in a co-creation environment that is fostered by human-AI collaboration. This relationship is especially clear in research and development, where AI speeds up the identification of novel substances, medications, and technological advancements.

2.2 Retraining and Enhancing Employee Skill Sets

Retraining and upskilling are necessary to equip the workforce for the future as automation and artificial intelligence (AI) transform the labor market.

Skills Gaps Identification

- **Workforce Analysis:** Companies need to perform in-depth investigations in order to pinpoint the skills gaps in their staff. This entails evaluating present competencies and contrasting them with those needed for new, automation- and AI-driven work opportunities.

- **Projecting Future Skills:** Companies can proactively identify the skills that will be in demand by projecting future market trends and technology breakthroughs. This kind of foresight makes it possible to create focused training initiatives to close these gaps.

Programs and Initiatives for Training

- **Personalized Training Plans:** Training curricula should be specifically tailored to address the skills gaps found in the workforce analysis. Both soft skills like problem-solving and critical thinking as well as technical abilities like programming and data analysis may be covered in these programs.

- **Virtual Education Platforms:** Online learning environments like Coursera, Udacity, and edX provide employees with accessible and adaptable training options. With the help of these platforms, employees may learn at their own pace and obtain the necessary credentials while taking classes on a variety of subjects.

Collaborations with Universities and Colleges

- **Partnerships with Educational Institutions:** Companies and academic institutions can collaborate to create curriculum that meets the demands of the business world. These collaborations guarantee that graduates have the know-how needed to prosper in an AI-driven economy.

- **Apprenticeships and Internships:** By providing internship and apprenticeship opportunities, educational institutions enable students to acquire real-world experience and important skills while still in school. Talent that is prepared to enter the workforce is created by these programs.

Industry and Government Support

- **Public-Private Partnerships:** Businesses in the public and private sectors can work together to finance and assist reskilling and upskilling programs. These collaborations may involve training subsidies, tax breaks, and grants to promote workforce development.

- **Programs for National Training:** Governments can put in place national training initiatives aimed at fostering expertise in fields with high demand, such data science, cybersecurity, and artificial intelligence. Community colleges, online platforms, and vocational institutions may all offer these programs.

2.3 The Creation of New Employment Positions: Data Analysts and AI Specialists

AI has led to the emergence of new job roles requiring specific knowledge and skills.

Experts in AI

- **Industry Researchers and Technologists:** These experts create AI systems, models, and algorithms. Their areas of focus include computer vision, natural language processing, machine learning, and other AI technologies. While AI developers usually work in industry to apply these improvements to real-world challenges, researchers frequently work in academic environments.

- **Engineers in Machine Learning:** Engineers that specialize in machine learning create and apply models that process and analyze data in order to generate forecasts or judgments. They handle big datasets, optimize algorithms, and implement models in real-world settings.

Data Scientists and Data Analysts

- **Data Scientists**: In order to produce insights that can be put into practice, data analysts must understand and analyze data. They assist firms in making defensible judgments by utilizing statistical methods and data visualization software. Data analysts frequently operate in a variety of sectors, such as marketing, finance, and healthcare.

- **Information Scientists:** Data scientists use intricate models to examine huge datasets and glean important insights. To find patterns and trends, they employ statistical techniques, machine learning algorithms, and programming abilities. The creation of recommendation engines, prediction models, and other AI applications depends heavily on data scientists.

Policy Experts and AI Ethicists

- **Ethicists:** As AI technologies proliferate, there is an increasing demand for experts who can handle AI's ethical ramifications. Bias, justice, accountability, transparency, and openness in AI systems are among the topics that AI ethicists study. They strive to guarantee responsible development and application of AI technologies.

- **Policy Specialists:** Experts in AI policy concentrate on establishing rules and laws for the moral application of AI. They collaborate with international groups, governments, and organizations to create frameworks that strike a balance between innovation and societal issues. Experts in policy are essential in building the legal and regulatory framework surrounding AI.

2.4 Flexible, Remote, and Automated Work in the Future

Driven by breakthroughs in AI and digital technology, the future of work will be characterized by more flexibility, remote operations, and automation.

Adaptable Work Schedules

- **Work from Home:** Since many professions may be completed outside of traditional office settings, the COVID-19 epidemic has expedited the acceptance of remote work. AI-powered project management software and video conferencing are examples of collaboration solutions that make remote work easier by facilitating smooth team coordination and communication.

- **Models of Hybrid Work:** Hybrid work models, which blend in-person and remote work, are becoming more and more popular in organizations. Employee freedom is increased with this strategy, which also preserves chances for face-to-face team development and cooperation.

Automation and Efficiency

- **Streamlining Regular Tasks with Automation:** Automation and artificial intelligence (AI) technology can handle monotonous and repetitive jobs, freeing up human workers to concentrate on more intricate and strategic work. Industries including manufacturing, logistics, and customer service are heavily reliant on automation.

- **Improved Tools for Productivity:** Productivity technologies driven by AI, such automated workflow systems and intelligent scheduling assistants, increase productivity and streamline corporate procedures. These technologies facilitate efficient job management, work prioritization, and teamwork among staff.

Diversity and Inclusion in the Workforce

- **Inclusive Hiring Procedures:** AI can assist businesses in locating and removing biases in their hiring procedures, fostering inclusion and diversity in the workplace. AI-powered hiring instruments review applications and evaluate applicants on the basis of their qualifications and skills rather than their subjective qualities.

- **Workplaces That Are Accessible:** Workplaces that are more accessible for people with disabilities can be made possible by AI technologies. AI-driven speech recognition and natural language processing capabilities, for instance, allow employees with speech or hearing impairments to communicate effectively.

Lifelong Learning:

- **Continuous Learning and Adaptation:** As technology advances more quickly than ever, workers must continue to learn in order to stay relevant. Employers need to encourage a culture of lifelong learning by giving staff members the chance to learn new things.

- **Self-adjustment and Hardiness:** Employees of the future must be flexible and resilient in the face of change. Companies should provide training, mentorship, and flexible career pathways to assist their employees in acquiring these skills.

The changing nature of the workplace is marked by a new

dynamic of human-AI collaboration, the need for reskilling and upskilling, the creation of new job roles, and the growing significance of automation, flexibility, and remote work. Organizations may foster a more inventive, productive, and inclusive work environment by embracing these changes.

CHAPTER 3

The Paradox of Automation

The workforce has changed significantly as a result of automation and artificial intelligence, presenting both opportunities and challenges.

3.1 Will Robots Take Away Our Jobs? Analyzing the Risks of Job Automation

One common concern is that automation and artificial intelligence would result in a large-scale loss of jobs. But the truth is more complicated than that.

Automation of Typical Tasks

- **Mundane and Repeated Jobs:** Automation and artificial intelligence are especially good at handling routine, repetitive, and rule-based jobs. It's common knowledge that jobs in manufacturing, data entry, and customer service are in danger since AI systems can perform these activities faster than humans.

Examples of Industries: Many manual labor jobs in manufacturing have been displaced by automated assembly lines and robotic arms. Artificial intelligence (AI) algorithms are used in the financial sector to reduce the need for human intervention by processing transactions and analyzing data.

Opening Up New Positions

- **Emerging Positions:** While certain industries are becoming automated, new positions in data science, robotics maintenance, and AI development are also being created. These new positions frequently offer prospects for career progression and call for higher skill levels.

- **Transformation of the Industry:** Automation is changing the way industries operate by generating a need for new goods and services. For instance, the popularity of autonomous vehicles is creating new positions in fleet management, software development, and vehicle design.

Change in the Type of Job

- **Augmented Roles:** Instead of being abolished, many professions are being altered. Human functions are enhanced by AI and automation, freeing up employees to concentrate on more complex jobs requiring creativity, problem-solving, and emotional intelligence.

- **Augmentation Examples:** AI helps medical professionals by evaluating imaging data and making recommendations for diagnosis, freeing up more time for patient care. Artificial intelligence (AI) solutions in the legal field simplify document analysis and research, freeing up attorneys to concentrate on case strategy and client relations.

3.2 The Gig Economy's Rise: Precarious Work and Flexibility

The advent of the gig economy has become a noteworthy feature of the contemporary labor market, partly due to technological progress.

Adaptability and Self-governance

- **Work-Life Harmony:** The gig economy improves

work-life balance by giving employees more freedom to choose when and where to work. Gig workers frequently have the freedom to choose their own hours and take on tasks that suit their qualifications and interests.

- **Diverse Possibilities:** Opportunities in a variety of fields, such as ride-sharing, freelancing writing, graphic design, and consultancy, are offered by the gig economy. Workers are able to investigate many career routes and multiple revenue sources thanks to this variety.

Precarious Work

- **Insecurity in Employment:** The gig economy is known for its flexibility, yet it is also frequently associated with unstable work circumstances. The employment security, benefits, and protections that traditional employees enjoy like health insurance, paid time off, and retirement plans are generally not available to gig workers.

- **The Volatility of Income:** Because gig employment is erratic in nature, income volatility affects freelance workers. Demand, the availability of gigs, and worker competition can all affect earnings, which can cause financial instability for individuals.

Policy and Regulatory Obstacles

Workplace Rights: The gig economy's growth has spurred debates concerning gig workers' rights to protection under the law. Regulations are being demanded by legislators and labor activists in order to guarantee gig workers' equitable pay, benefits, and working conditions.

Regulation Examples: Certain regions have implemented policies aimed at offering fundamental safeguards to independent contractors. Assembly Bill 5 (AB5) in California, for example, seeks to reclassify some gig workers as employees, giving them access to benefits and protections.

3.3 The Human Advantage: Critical Thinking, Social Skills, and Creativity

Even with AI and automation's powers, humans have certain benefits that are unmatched by machines.

Intellect and Originality

- **Imaginative Approach to Solving Problems:** In the workplace, human ingenuity is still a valuable resource. AI is not very good at thinking creatively, coming up with original ideas, or approaching problems from multiple perspectives.

- **Creative Remedies:** Human creativity is vital to many industries, including entertainment, design, and advertising. While artificial intelligence (AI) can help with certain activities, such as data analysis and content creation, human expertise is often needed for creative direction and innovation.

Evaluative Reasoning and Thinking

- **Intricate Decision-Making:** Humans need critical thinking and judgment to make complex decisions based on ethical considerations, experience, and context. On the other side, AI is unable to comprehend ambiguity and subtlety and frequently depends on pre-established rules.

- **Coordinated Planning:** Strategic planning-related roles, like project management and executive leadership, need for the application of critical thinking skills and the capacity to weigh long-term effects. Human leaders succeed in these domains by incorporating various viewpoints and adjusting to evolving situations.

In many jobs, interpersonal skills such as empathy, communication, and teamwork are essential, and here is where social and emotional intelligence comes in. Effective cooperation, dispute resolution, and relationship-building are made possible by these abilities, which are difficult for AI to imitate.

- **consumer engagement:** Human social skills are extremely beneficial in jobs involving consumer engagement, such as sales, counseling, and healthcare. While AI can help with administrative and data processing duties, human interaction is still necessary to establish trust and comprehend client needs.

3.4 Education's Significance: Adjusting to a Shifting Labor Market

To adjust to the changing labor market brought about by

automation and artificial intelligence, education and lifelong learning are essential.

Eternal Education

- **Ongoing Skill Advancement:** In order to remain relevant as technology advances, professionals need to pursue lifelong learning. Adapting to new tasks and responsibilities requires ongoing skill development through formal schooling, online courses, and on-the-job training.

- **Entrepreneurial and Personal Development:** In addition to improving job opportunities, lifelong learning promotes intellectual curiosity and personal development. People who have a constant learning mindset are better equipped to handle job changes and take advantage of new chances.

STEM Education:

- STEM stands for science, technology, engineering, and math. Students who have a strong STEM education are more prepared for professions in artificial intelligence, data science, and other technology-related fields. Early exposure to STEM topics can stimulate curiosity and increase one's competence in these fields.

- **Multidisciplinary Education:** Holistic learning is promoted by integrating STEM education with other academic fields like the humanities and social sciences. This multidisciplinary method encourages creativity, critical thinking, and problem-solving skills for difficult, real-world situations.

Digital Literacy

- **Introductory Digital Competencies:** All workers must possess a basic level of digital literacy in an increasingly digital world. Being able to use digital tools, comprehend cybersecurity, and navigate online platforms are essential abilities for anyone looking to work in the modern workforce.

- **High Level Technical Proficiency**: Advanced technical abilities, such as programming, data analysis, and machine learning, are essential for anybody wishing to work in the technology industry. These abilities can be acquired by people with the aid of specialized training courses and credentials.

Developing Soft Skills

- **Partnership and Communication:** In today's workplace, soft skills like leadership, cooperation, and communication are becoming more and more crucial. The development of these abilities should be emphasized in education and training programs in order to get students ready for dynamic, team-oriented workplaces.

- **Self-adjustment and Hardiness:** In a labor market that is changing quickly, the capacity for change adaptation and failure recovery is essential. Education systems ought to prioritize helping students develop their capacity for resilience, adaptability, and problem-solving.

The automation conundrum draws attention to the dual character of AI's influence on the workforce, where chances for new positions and the advantages of human expertise coexist with the possibility of job displacement. People and businesses may successfully navigate the shifting labor market and prosper in the age of artificial intelligence and automation by embracing lifelong learning, placing a strong emphasis on STEM and digital literacy, and cultivating soft skills.

CHAPTER 4

THE FRAMEWORK OF POLICIES

Artificial intelligence (AI) is bringing about a number of policy concerns that need to be addressed in order to ensure sustainable, ethical, and egalitarian development as it continues to revolutionize economies and sectors. The regulation of AI to address ethical issues and bias, the idea of Universal Basic Income (UBI) as a potential safety net for displaced workers, the roles of the government and educational institutions in reskilling initiatives, and the updating of labor laws to the AI era are just a few of the important policy areas that are covered in this chapter.

4.1 AI Regulation: Ethical Issues and Prejudice

Because of AI's rapid development, thorough regulation is required to address ethical issues and reduce biases that could have a big influence on society.

AI Ethics Frameworks

- **Accountability and Transparency:** A key component of ethical AI frameworks is the requirement for system transparency. This includes thorough documentation of the creation, training, and application of AI algorithms. Accountability mechanisms guarantee that organizations using AI systems can be held accountable for their deeds and results.

- **Discrimination-free and Fairness**: Fairness and nondiscrimination must be incorporated into AI system design. To find and reduce biases in AI algorithms, extensive testing is required. Diverse data sets should be included, according to ethical rules, to lessen the possibility of biased results that disproportionately harm underrepresented populations.

AI System Bias

- **Bias Sources:** A number of factors, such as skewed training data, poor algorithm design, and ingrained human preconceptions in the data, can lead to bias in AI systems. These prejudices may produce unfair results in the employment, credit, and law enforcement sectors.

- **Reduction Techniques:** A multifaceted strategy is needed to mitigate bias, including the development of bias-detection technologies, frequent audits of AI systems, and the acquisition of varied and representative data. Strong solutions require cooperation between ethicists, regulatory agencies, and AI developers.

Legislative Measures:

- **Regulatory Approaches:** Governments from all around the world are thinking about enacting laws to control AI. These actions could involve setting up oversight organizations, developing criteria for AI development and application, and enforcing adherence to moral standards.

- **Collaboration on a global scale:** Since AI research is a multinational endeavor, international cooperation is essential to the creation of unified regulatory standards. International frameworks to support ethical AI are being developed by organizations like the European Union and the

United Nations.

4.2 The Universal Basic Income: A Shield for the Labor Force That Is Being Replaced?

The idea of a Universal Basic Income (UBI) as a way to give displaced people financial security has gained traction in light of the potential for AI and automation to replace jobs.

Understanding UBI

- **Definition and guiding principles:** A proposed program known as Universal Basic Income (UBI) would provide all residents, regardless of income or job status, with a regular, unconditional payment from the government. Universality, unconditionality, and regularity are the tenets of the UBI.
- **Securing the Economy:** The main objective of universal basic income (UBI) is to guarantee that everyone has a minimum income to cover their basic requirements, thereby reducing poverty and promoting economic security. This may lessen the financial volatility brought on by automation and

artificial intelligence-related job displacement.

Benefits of Universal Basic Income

- **Reduction of Poverty:** By giving every individual a reliable source of income, universal basic income (UBI) can drastically reduce poverty. This can raise living standards and lessen the need for government assistance programs.

- **Inflationary Pressures:** UBI can boost economic activity by giving citizens more money to spend on products and services, which could result in the development of jobs in other industries.

Difficulties and Rebuttals

- **Sustainability and Funding:** Financing is one of the main obstacles to the implementation of UBI. To achieve UBI without seriously disrupting the economy, policymakers must find sustainable sources of funding.

- **Incentives for Work:** Opponents contend that if the basic income is enough to cover all necessities, the universal basic income (UBI) may lessen the incentive to work. In response, supporters argue that universal basic income (UBI) can give people the freedom to pursue fulfilling careers, further their education, and launch their own businesses.

Research and Pilot Programs

- **International Experiments:** Several nations have carried up pilot projects to evaluate the viability and effects of universal basic income. Important information about the effects of UBI on employment, well-being, and economic activity is provided by these experiments.

- **Research on Policy:** To comprehend the long-term impacts of universal basic income and to improve policy designs, more research is necessary. This entails evaluating the wider economic ramifications as well as the effects on various demographic groupings.

4.3 Initiatives for Reskilling: The Roles of Government and Education

Initiatives aimed at reskilling workers are essential for preparing them for the automation and artificial intelligence that will change the nature of employment. In these endeavors, the government and academic institutions are essential.

Programs for Reskilling Led by the Government

- **Public-Private Partnerships:** Governments and private businesses can work together to develop reskilling initiatives that are specific to the needs of the industry. These collaborations can offer capital, materials, and knowledge to create training programs that work.

- **Rewards and Subsidies:** Governments can provide tax breaks, grants, and subsidies, among other incentives, to promote involvement in reskilling initiatives. These financial aid options can lessen the financial strain on people and organizations making training investments.

Educational Institutions' Role

- **Updates to the Curriculum:** Academic institutions need to revise their courses to incorporate competencies necessary for the AI-driven labor market. This entails incorporating topics like machine learning, data science, and AI ethics into already-existing applications.

- **Prospects for Lifelong Learning:** With the help of adult education programs, certification schemes, and online courses, universities and institutions can provide chances for lifelong learning. People may balance employment and other obligations while acquiring new skills thanks to these flexible learning options.

Training Specific to the Industry

- **Personalized Programs:** Programs for reskilling should be customized to meet the unique requirements of various industries. Workers in manufacturing, for instance, could need to learn about robotics and automation technology, while healthcare professionals might need to be trained in AI-driven diagnoses.

- **Cooperative Methods:** Educational institutions and professional associations can work together to create and implement training programs that are specifically tailored to the needs of the students. This guarantees that the instruction is current and adheres to industry norms.

Evaluating Achievement

- **Results and Influence:** The results and effects of reskilling programs on employment rates, income levels, and work satisfaction should be used to gauge their effectiveness. To pinpoint areas in need of development and confirm that the programs are accomplishing their goals, ongoing observation and assessment are crucial.

- **Comments and Modifications:** Retraining programs must be improved and adjusted based on input from participants and industry stakeholders. By using an iterative process, the training is guaranteed to stay current and useful in meeting the changing demands of the labor market.

4.4 Labor Laws in the Future: Getting Ready for the AI Era

Labor laws must be updated in the AI era to safeguard workers' rights and promote fair labor practices, given the advent of automation and artificial intelligence.

Redefining Employment Status:

- **Updating Employment Definitions:** Gig workers, independent contractors, and people performing AI-augmented work might not be sufficiently included in traditional definitions of employment. To give these workers protections, such as access to benefits and job stability, labor laws must be modified.

- **Adaptability and Safety:** Flexibility and protections should be balanced in new employment definitions. For instance, gig workers ought to be able to select their own work schedules and be eligible for benefits like health insurance and retirement plans.

Worker Rights and Protections

- **Fair Wages:** Labor laws ought to provide equitable compensation for all workers, including independent contractors and gig workers. This entails setting minimum wage guidelines and dealing with problems like unpaid overtime and wage fraud.

- **Wellness and Security:** Automation and artificial

intelligence (AI) raise new concerns for worker health and safety. Labor regulations need to address these dangers by establishing guidelines for the responsible use of AI technology and making sure that employees receive the necessary training to safely operate and interact with these systems.

Collaborative Dispute Settlement and Representation

- **Organization and Promotion:** Workers ought to be able to form unions and participate in collective bargaining, especially in fields where automation and artificial intelligence play a significant role. To safeguard the interests of employees, labor laws ought to encourage the creation of unions and worker advocacy organizations.

- **Online Resources:** Labor regulations must take into account the special difficulties that come with the increasing amount of work that is mediated through digital platforms. This entails making sure platform mechanisms are transparent and provide channels for resolving conflicts to employees.

International Labor Standards:

- **Global Considerations:** Due to the global nature of automation and artificial intelligence, international cooperation is needed to create labor norms that safeguard workers everywhere. The International Labour Organization (ILO) is one organization that can be very important in establishing and advancing these standards.

- **Working Across Borders:** The ramifications of cross-border employment, in which employees in one nation work for employers in another, must also be taken into account by labor regulations. This involves resolving matters among many authorities, such as social security, taxes, and labor rights.

The policy landscape for AI entails tackling moral issues, guaranteeing financial stability with programs like universal basic income, encouraging reskilling efforts, and modifying labor laws to safeguard workers in the AI age. In the era of automation and artificial intelligence, governments and institutions can contribute to the creation of a more sustainable and fair future by addressing these policy issues.

CHAPTER 5

The View From A Global Angle

Not everyone is affected equally by artificial intelligence (AI), which is changing economies and society all around the world. Critical issues to solve include the gap between rich and developing countries, the automation of global supply chains, the difficulties facing infrastructure in becoming ready for the digital era, and the significance of international cooperation. This chapter offers a thorough examination of these problems and how they affect our increasingly interconnected world.

5.1 Developed vs. Developing Countries: AI's Different Effects

Although artificial intelligence (AI) has significantly advanced science and technology, rich and poor countries have different experiences with its advantages and disadvantages.

Technological Progress and Economic Divides

- **Resource Accessibility:** Developed countries can embrace and use AI technology more successfully because they have easier access to capital, cutting-edge research facilities, and trained personnel. On the other hand, underdeveloped countries frequently face resource constraints that make it difficult for them to use AI to drive economic progress.

- **Readiness of Infrastructure:** Better digital infrastructure, such as fast internet, dependable power, and sophisticated telecommunications networks, is generally found in developed nations. The implementation and scalability of AI systems depend on this infrastructure, which developing countries may lack in substantial amounts.

Workforce Dynamics and Employment

- **Job Displacement:** Automation and artificial intelligence (AI) are projected to displace low-skilled, repetitive occupations in industrialized countries, displacing workers in industries like manufacturing and retail. To lessen the effects, these nations frequently have strong social safety nets and reskilling initiatives.

- **Demand for Work and Economic Growth:** AI may help developing countries by increasing productivity and generating new employment opportunities, especially in technology-driven industries. These advantages might not materialize completely, and there is still a chance that unemployment and inequality would worsen in the absence of sufficient laws and training initiatives.

Regulatory and Policy Difficulties

- **Regulatory Structures:** Developed countries are more likely to have frameworks in place for regulations to handle the moral and legal ramifications of artificial intelligence. These frameworks can lessen bias, safeguard data privacy, and enable ethical AI implementation. Developing countries might not have complete rules, which exposes them to hazards related to ethics and security.

- **International Standards:** International trade and collaboration are hindered by the absence of consistent global standards for artificial intelligence. Developed countries frequently take the lead in establishing these benchmarks, but in order to produce inclusive and equitable policies, poor countries must be included in the discussion.

5.2 Global Supply Chains and the Rise of Automation in Manufacturing

Global supply networks are changing, and manufacturing processes are being revolutionized by AI-driven automation.

Automation and Production Efficiency

- **Smart Factories:** The fusion of artificial intelligence (AI) with automation in the manufacturing sector has given rise to "smart factories," which are networked machines and systems that continuously optimize production processes. As a consequence, operational expenses are decreased, downtime is decreased, and efficiency is raised.

- **Quality Control:** AI-powered QCS systems employ

machine learning algorithms to find irregularities and flaws in products, guaranteeing improved standards and cutting down on waste. This makes producers more competitive in international markets.

The impact of nearshoring and reshoring on global supply chains Reshoring or nearshoring manufacturing operations is something developed corporations may think about as automation lessens the dependency on cheap labor. This can increase supply chain resilience, shorten supply chains, and save transportation expenses.

- **Visibility of Supply Chain:** Predictive analytics and blockchain are two examples of AI technologies that increase supply chain visibility and transparency. This makes it possible for businesses to anticipate changes in demand, better manage inventories, and react to interruptions.

Difficulties and Aspects to Take into Account

- **Replacement of Workers:** Automation may result in workforce displacement, especially in areas where manufacturing employment is highly concentrated. Implementing reskilling and upskilling programs is essential to assisting workers in adjusting to new jobs in the dynamic labor market.

- **Differences in Economics:** The economic divide between areas that can afford to invest in cutting-edge technologies and others that cannot be made worse by automation. To alleviate these discrepancies, policymakers should encourage the adoption of inclusive economic policies and provide assistance for the use of technology in underprivileged communities.

5.3 Infrastructure's Challenge: Gearing Up for the Digital Era

Creating the required infrastructure is crucial to use AI to its maximum potential and getting ready for the digital era.

Development of Digital Infrastructure

- **High-Speed Internet**: Using AI technologies fundamentally requires having access to high-speed internet. Expanding broadband networks requires funding from the public and commercial sectors, especially in underserved and rural areas.

- **Data Centers**: Massive volumes of data must be processed and stored in robust data centers due to the rise of AI applications. To enable AI-driven breakthroughs, developing countries must invest in the construction and modernization of data centers.

Electricity and Networking

- **Stable Energy Source:** Artificial intelligence (AI) systems, especially those that analyze massive amounts of data, need a steady and dependable energy source. You can guarantee continuous operations by updating power infrastructure and investing in renewable energy sources.

- **Networks for Telecommunication:** 5G and other advanced telecommunications networks are essential for providing the low latency and connection that AI applications demand. In order to expedite the development of these networks, telecom companies and governments must work together.

Education and Human Capital

- **STEM Education:** To propel AI innovation, we need a workforce that is highly educated and possesses strong STEM (Science, Technology, Engineering, and Mathematics) competencies. Institutions of higher learning must place a strong emphasis on STEM subjects and offer AI-related training.

- **Technical Proficiency:** Beyond technical expertise, digital literacy is essential for the general public to comprehend and make good use of AI technologies. Community initiatives and public awareness campaigns can aid in closing the digital literacy gap.

5.4 Promoting Global Cooperation: Exchange of Best Practices and Knowledge

In order to solve global issues and maximize the advantages of AI, international cooperation is essential.

Research and Knowledge Sharing

- **Collaborative Research:** International cooperation in AI research can hasten scientific progress and encourage the creation of moral AI. Facilitating the interchange of ideas and expertise are joint research efforts, academic alliances, and knowledge-sharing platforms.

- **Data Sharing and Open Access:** Ensuring that discoveries benefit a wider audience and democratizing AI development can be achieved through open access to research findings and data sets. Institutions and governments should support laws that protect security and privacy while fostering open data exchange.

International Ethics and Standards

- **Unifying Standards:** Global trade and cooperation can be facilitated by creating standardized AI standards. These standards are largely established by international bodies like the International Telecommunication Union and the United Nations.

- **Ethical Principles:** Global ethical standards for AI development and application can guarantee responsible technology development and application. Globally, collaborative efforts can solve challenges like accountability, transparency, and bias.

Technical Support and Capacity Building

- **Aiding Developing Countries:** Developed countries

may help poor countries realize the potential of AI by offering technical support and capacity-building assistance. This involves bridging the digital divide through the provision of capital, know-how, and technology transfer.

- **International Investment and Aid:** Financing infrastructure projects and reskilling initiatives in underdeveloped countries can be greatly aided by international aid groups and development banks. The global AI environment can be made more egalitarian and inclusive through strategic investments.

Comprehending the global viewpoint on AI entails realizing the disparate effects on developed and developing countries, the evolution of global supply chains and manufacturing, the difficulties in constructing the required infrastructure, and the significance of promoting international cooperation. We can build a more sustainable and inclusive future in the era of artificial intelligence by tackling these issues.

CHAPTER 6

THE ROLE OF HUMANITY IN AI AGE

It is critical to keep the human element in mind as automation and artificial intelligence (AI) continue to change the workplace. This chapter looks at how work is being redefined, how important soft skills are, what the future holds for leisure, and how to create a workplace that is focused on people. We can make sure that the incorporation of AI improves human well-being and fosters a more creative and happy work environment by concentrating on these areas.

6.1 Redefining Work: In an Automated World, Meaning and Purpose

When ordinary jobs can be performed by machines, the definition of work is changing. The emphasis is moving from jobs that are only functional to ones that have meaning and purpose.

Changing Job Roles

- **Strategic and Creative Roles:** There is an increasing need for people in positions requiring creativity, strategic thinking, and problem-solving skills as automation replaces repetitive work. The importance of jobs in design, innovation, and strategic planning is rising.

- **Services Focused on People:** Personal contact-based jobs like those in healthcare, education, and customer service are becoming more and more in demand. These jobs involve communication skills, sensitivity, and a thorough comprehension of human needs.

Work Driven by Purpose

- **Value Alignment:** Workers are looking for positions that support a greater good in society and coincide with their personal ideals. The modern workforce is drawn to companies that prioritize sustainability and corporate social responsibility.

- **Workplace Engagement and Satisfaction:** Increased engagement and job happiness are the results of meaningful work. Employees are more driven and effective when they believe that their job is making a difference.

Lifelong Learning:

- **Continuous Learning and Growth:** The speed at which technology is changing demands constant learning and skill improvement. To be current and flexible, employees should be encouraged to pursue lifelong learning.

- **Individual Growth:** Initiatives for personal growth including workshops, mentoring programs, and resource access should be supported by organizations. Putting money into staff development promotes a continuous improvement culture.

6.2 The Value of Soft Skills: Empathy, Cooperation, and Communication

In the AI era, soft skills are becoming more and more important, even while technical abilities are still crucial. Effective communication and teamwork are essential for success in today's technologically sophisticated business, and these abilities make this possible.

Interaction:

- **Effective Communication:** Effective and transparent communication is essential to teamwork and project success. Workers need to be able to express themselves clearly, offer criticism, and have fruitful conversations.

- **Digital correspondence:** Digital communication abilities are crucial as the amount of work done remotely increases. Effective use of platforms and tools for communication guarantees smooth collaboration across teams that are spread out geographically.

Cooperation

- **Group Dynamics:** Innovation and problem-solving require teamwork. Workers need to be able to collaborate well with others in order to accomplish shared objectives by utilizing a variety of viewpoints and abilities.

- **Interaction Across Functional Domains:** Cross-functional teamwork is crucial in a complex business setting. To move projects forward, employees must be able to collaborate with coworkers from many departments and disciplines.

Compassion

- **Comprehending Others:** Employees with empathy are able to comprehend and relate to the feelings and viewpoints of others. This ability is essential for creating a great work atmosphere and solid partnerships.

- **Client-First Strategy:** Understanding client demands and providing great service also require empathy. A customer-focused strategy increases loyalty and satisfaction.

6.3 The Future of Leisure: Time for Individual Development and Creativity

There is a chance to reconsider how we spend our free time as automation cuts down on the amount of time spent on repetitive jobs. Increased creativity, personal development, and general wellbeing can result from this change.

Creativity and Innovation

- **Creative Pursuits:** People who have more free time can pursue hobbies, music, art, and other creative endeavors. These pursuits stimulate creativity and enhance individual satisfaction.

- **Incubation of Innovation:** New ideas and breakthroughs can germinate during leisure time. People who are free to pursue their hobbies can come up with original ideas and answers.

Emotional Development

- **Technical Proficiency:** Self-improvement and skill development are opportunities that come with spare time. To improve their skills, people can undertake personal initiatives, certificates, and courses.

- **Wellness and Health:** One can devote leisure time to improving one's physical and mental health. A happier and more balanced life is facilitated by practices like meditation, physical activity, and quality time spent with loved ones.

Involvement in the Community

- **Volunteerism:** Having more free time allows people to volunteer and support their communities.

Volunteering improves social ties and creates a feeling of purpose.

- **Relationships with Others:** Social ties can be established and maintained during leisure time. Robust social networks are necessary for both general happiness and emotional support.

6.4 Human-Centered Workplace: Promoting Health and Creativity

Encouraging an innovative culture and optimizing employee well-being require a human-centered workplace.

Well-Being of Employees

- **Work-Life Harmony:** Work-life balance is a top priority for organizations in order to guard against burnout and guarantee employee wellbeing. A better work environment is facilitated by time-off regulations, remote work opportunities, and flexible work schedules.
- **Help for Mental Health:** It is essential to provide resources and support for mental health. Employee support efforts, counseling services, and wellness

programs can aid with stress management and mental health maintenance.

Diversity and Inclusion

- **Inclusive and Diverse Work Environment:** Creativity and innovation are encouraged in a diverse and inclusive workplace. Employers ought to actively encourage diversity in the employment process, develop inclusive policies, and guarantee that every employee has equal access to opportunities.

- **Support and Belonging:** Encouraging a feeling of support and belonging is crucial for retaining employees. A positive work culture is facilitated by employee resource groups, mentoring programs, and inclusive leadership techniques.

Creativity and Innovation

- **Encouraging Innovation:** Businesses should foster a culture that rewards creativity and taking calculated risks. This entails giving staff members the tools, time, and encouragement they need to experiment with novel concepts and inventive solutions.

- **Collaborative Spaces:** It's critical to create collaborative workspaces that encourage communication and the exchange of ideas. Innovation centers, open office plans, and online collaboration platforms can improve creativity and teamwork.

Culture and Leadership

- **Transformational Leadership:** Employees are inspired and motivated by transformational leaders who cultivate a culture of continuous development and foster a common vision. Fostering innovation and organizational change requires strong leadership.

- **Culture of Organization:** It is crucial to have an innovative, collaborative, and well-empowered workplace culture. It is imperative for leaders to proactively foster and strengthen this culture by their deeds and directives.

There are a lot of opportunities to redefine work, highlight the value of soft skills, reconsider leisure time, and establish a human-centered workplace as a result of the integration of AI and automation in the workplace. Organizations may make sure that technological improvements improve human well-being and foster a more creative and happy work environment by concentrating on these areas.

CHAPTER 7

INEQUALITY AND THE AI REVOLUTION

As artificial intelligence (AI) changes enterprises and the labor market, it is posing significant challenges about inequality. The potential for AI to widen the skills gap, the significance of equitable access to education, the debate over universal basic income as a social justice tool, and the necessity of tackling the digital divide to ensure inclusive AI development are all covered in this chapter. By addressing these problems, we can work toward an AI-driven future that is advantageous to all parties.

7.1 The Growing Skills Divide: The Potential to Become More Inequitable

Artificial intelligence (AI) and automation technologies are developing at a rapid pace, which could exacerbate already-existing job disparities by expanding the skills gap.

Skill Requirements and Technological Advancements

- **Emerging Skill Demands:** The need for advanced technological skills like data science, machine learning, and robotics is being driven by automation and artificial intelligence. But a small percentage of the workforce often possesses these talents.

- **Routine Job Obsolescence:** Many old positions are becoming outdated as routine and manual jobs become more automated. These workers might not have the abilities to move into new roles.

Differences in Income

- **Inequality of Income:** There could be a rise in income disparity as highly skilled individuals demand premium salaries. People who are deprived of possibilities for education and training could be at a disadvantage.

- **Differences in Location:** In the AI era, areas with robust technical infrastructure and educational institutions will be better positioned to prosper, while other regions may fall behind and thereby widen regional disparities.

Lifelong Learning Initiatives:

- **Mitigating the Skills Gap:** It is crucial to promote lifetime learning and ongoing skill development. Employers, governments, and educational institutions must work together to offer accessible learning opportunities.

- **Asset Management and Vocational Training:** Increasing the number of apprenticeship and vocational training programs can assist people in gaining real-world skills that are pertinent to the changing employment market.

7.2 Education Access: Preparing Everyone for the Workforce of the Future

Fair access to education is essential for equipping people for the workforce of the future in an AI-driven economy.

Equity in Education

- **Everyone's Access to High-Quality Education:** It is essential to make sure that everyone has early access to high-quality education. This entails making investments in public education systems and minimizing inequalities in access to learning materials.

- **Education in STEM:** Putting a strong emphasis on STEM (science, technology, engineering, and mathematics) education is essential to preparing students for careers in AI.

Retraining and Adult Education

- **Programs for Continuing Education**: For workers whose employment is at risk of automation, opportunities for adult education and retraining are critical. These courses ought to be accessible and reasonably priced.
- **Virtual Education Platforms:** By enabling people to learn at their own speed and from any location, the use of online learning platforms helps democratize access to education.

To design and support education projects, governments, educational institutions, and private sector groups must work together in public-private partnerships. Innovation in training and education can be fostered by public-private collaborations.

- **Industry-University Partnership:** Involving experts in the industry in the curriculum development process guarantees that educational initiatives are in line with the capabilities that employers are looking for.

7.3 Universal Basic Income: An Instrument for Gender Parity?

In the era of artificial intelligence, the idea of a universal basic income (UBI) has gained popularity as a potential remedy for economic inequality.

Understanding Universal Basic Income

- **Basic Financial stability:** UBI entails giving every citizen a fixed amount of money on a regular basis, without conditions, in order to guarantee a minimal degree of financial stability. This has the potential to lessen income inequality and poverty.
- **Assisting Relocated Workers:** UBI can act as a safety net for impacted workers when automation replaces some job roles, freeing them up to seek further education, training, or entrepreneurial

endeavors.

Issues Regarding the Impact of UBI

- **Economic Sustainability:** Opponents claim that the expense of widely implementing UBI might be unaffordable. Investigating financial sources, including tax revisions, is crucial to ensuring the sustainability of the economy.

- **Rewards and Inspiration:** There is worry that a universal basic income could make people less motivated to work. Proponents contend, however, that it can free people from the burden of financial uncertainty to pursue fulfilling careers and personal growth.

Global Experiments:

- **Pilot Programs and Evidence:** Pilot projects have been carried out in a number of nations and areas to evaluate the viability and effects of universal basic income. These studies offer insightful information about the possible advantages and difficulties of it.

- **Assessing Results:** To determine how UBI pilot programs would affect employment rates, overall well-being, and the eradication of poverty, a thorough evaluation is required.

7.4 Concluding the Digital Gap: Guaranteeing Inclusive AI Progress

Inclusive AI development depends on ensuring that all people and communities have access to digital technology.

Infrastructure and Digital Access

- **Internet Connectivity:** Having inexpensive and dependable internet access is essential for taking part in the digital economy. Expanding internet connection to underprivileged communities is something that needs to be done.
- **Technology Available:** Access to digital tools and devices is necessary for people to participate in online employment, education, and entrepreneurship. This covers programs aimed at providing subsidized or reasonably priced equipment.

Digital Literacy

- **Introductory Digital Competencies:** Encouraging

digital literacy is essential to equipping people to use the digital environment. Basic digital literacy should be emphasized in educational programs, including how to use computers, access the internet, and comprehend online security.

- **High Level Digital Proficiencies:** In addition to fundamental abilities, people need to possess sophisticated digital capabilities including data analysis, coding, and digital content creation.

Diverse Representation

- **Inclusive AI Development:** To build inclusive and objective AI systems, it is imperative that development teams for AI have a broad representation of members. Biases in AI systems can be found and lessened with the assistance of diverse viewpoints.

- **Intelligent AI Methods:** AI technologies are used ethically and benefit all societal segments when ethical criteria for AI development are developed and followed. This covers the justice, accountability, and transparency of AI systems.

Involvement in the Community

- **Local Projects:** Initiatives from the community can be very helpful in closing the digital divide. Digital training and support services can be offered via neighborhood associations, libraries, and community centers.

- **Awareness-Building Initiatives:** Increasing people's understanding of the value of digital inclusion and the resources at their disposal can motivate more people to take part in digital projects.

Tackling the issues of inequality in the AI era calls for a diverse strategy. We can move toward an AI-driven future that is inclusive and egalitarian by concentrating on bridging the digital divide, guaranteeing equitable access to education, investigating the possibility of universal basic income, and closing the skills gap. It is the joint responsibility of policymakers, educators, and business executives to establish a welcoming atmosphere that enables every person to prosper in the dynamic labor market.

CHAPTER 8

AI's Ethical Consequences

Artificial intelligence (AI) presents unprecedented opportunities for efficiency and creativity, but it also raises important ethical concerns. This chapter examines the ethical implications of AI, paying particular emphasis to minimizing algorithmic bias, preserving explainability and transparency, addressing the human cost of automation, and advocating for a human-centered approach to the future of work.

8.1 Algorithm Bias: Reducing Discrimination in Artificial Intelligence Systems

Despite their strength, AI systems have the potential to unintentionally reinforce biases found in training sets, producing biased results.

Cognizing Algorithmic Bias
- **Types and Definitions:** Systematic and unfair

discrimination in AI systems is referred to as algorithmic bias. It can take many different forms, including class, gender, and racial bias.

- **Basis Reasons:** Bias in AI is frequently caused by poorly designed algorithms, biased training data, or inadvertent connections that reinforce preexisting social preconceptions.

Reducing Prejudice

- **Acquiring and Arranging Data**: Reducing bias requires ensuring that training data is representative and diverse. Procedures for gathering data should be open and transparent, with steps taken to detect and lessen bias.

- **Equity Algorithm:** Prior to AI model deployment, bias in the models can be identified and reduced with the use of testing frameworks and fairness measures. Methods like fairness-aware learning algorithms and debiasing algorithms are under development.

- **Review of Ethics:** Interdisciplinary teams can detect potential biases and ethical issues early in the development process by conducting ethical evaluations of AI systems.

Legal and Regulatory Structures

- **Laws Preventing Discrimination:** Individuals impacted by prejudiced algorithms may be able to seek legal action by having AI systems adhere to current anti-discrimination laws. Additionally, new laws that explicitly address AI prejudice are being considered by policymakers.

- **Accountability and Auditing:** It is crucial to set up procedures for evaluating AI systems and holding programmers responsible for skewed results. This fosters responsible AI deployment and transparency.

8.2 Explainability and Transparency: Developing Reputable AI Tools

AI systems' lack of explainability and transparency has the potential to erode public confidence and prevent broad adoption.

Importance of Transparency

- **User Trust:** By revealing how AI systems function and make judgments, transparency increases user trust. If users are aware of the underlying mechanisms, they are more inclined to accept recommendations made by AI.

- **Responsibility:** Systems with transparent AI enable supervision and accountability. Stakeholders are able to assess the dependability and fairness of AI choices and take appropriate action if needed.

AI Explainability

- **Comprehensible Models:** It is essential to create interpretable AI models that offer precise justifications for their judgments. Explainability can be improved by using strategies like feature importance analysis and model visualization.

- **Introductory Knowledge:** Contextual explanations aid users in comprehending the reasoning behind the conclusions or suggestions made by AI systems. Input data, methods, and criteria for making decisions are all described in depth.

Difficulties and Solutions

- **Complexity vs. Explainability**: It can be difficult to strike a balance between the complexity of AI algorithms and the requirement for explainability. Scholars are investigating methods for decomposing intricate models without compromising their correctness.

- **Educating Stakeholders:** Spreading knowledge about AI technologies and their ramifications to users, legislators, and the general public encourages ethical AI adoption and helps people make educated decisions.

8.3 The Social Impact and Job Losses Associated with Automation's Human Cost

Artificial intelligence (AI)-driven automation has the potential to upend businesses, eliminate jobs, and create serious socio economic problems.

Impact on Employment

- **Job Displacement:** Automating routine and manual labor puts workers at danger of losing their jobs and facing unstable finances.
- The adoption of AI results in a **skill shift** as new employment roles requiring sophisticated technical

abilities are created; this could exacerbate the skills gap and increase income inequality.

Contextual Considerations

- **Inequality of Income:** If benefits are not dispersed fairly or if there are no possibilities for displaced people to retrain or re-skill, automation may make income inequality worse.
- **Intellectual Unity:** Resolving the issue of automation-related job losses is essential to preserving social harmony and averting civil upheaval. Policies that assist impacted workers can lessen their detrimental effects on society.

The implementation of labor market policies, such as career counseling, job training programs, and unemployment insurance, can serve as a means of mitigating the adverse impacts of automation.

- **Universal Basic Income:** Some support UBI as a safety net for displaced workers, offering monetary stability and encouraging entrepreneurship and economic resilience.

8.4 A Human-Centered Perspective on the Future of Work

In the middle of AI's transformative potential, it is crucial to prioritize human well-being and ethical behavior by taking a human-centered approach to the future of work.

Human-Centered Workplace

- **Workplace Well-Being:** Promoting work-life balance, flexible scheduling, and mental health support for employees all contribute to a happy and effective workplace.
- **Inclusive Employment Practices:** Promoting diversity, equity, and inclusion in recruiting procedures encourages a workforce that is diverse and lessens prejudices in the use of AI.

The responsible deployment of AI technology in accordance with society values is ensured by the formulation and observance of ethical norms for AI development. This covers the values of responsibility, transparency, justice, and privacy.

- **Involvement with Stakeholders:** Involving

stakeholders in the creation of AI, such as workers, customers, legislators, and community leaders, encourages ethical and inclusive decision-making.

The promotion of ethical literacy among AI developers, users, and the general public can lead to responsible AI adoption and reduce possible hazards. This is achieved through Public Awareness and Education.

- **Ongoing Conversation:** Encouraging continuous communication and cooperation between interested parties guarantees that moral issues change as technology develops and as society demands them to.

Taking proactive steps to reduce prejudice, improve explainability and transparency, prevent job displacement, and advance a human-centered vision for the future of work is necessary to address the ethical concerns of AI. We can harness the revolutionary potential of AI while preserving societal values and fostering equitable prosperity if ethics are given top priority in AI development and deployment.

CHAPTER 9

OUR CHOICE FOR THE FUTURE

When imagining how artificial intelligence (AI) will change the future, important choices need to be made to direct its effects in a constructive direction. This chapter examines the ways in which legislation, education, innovation, and teamwork can influence the nature of employment in the future, utilize technology to advance human welfare, encourage inclusive development, and promote sustainability.

9.1 Creating the Future of Workplace Innovation, Policy, and Education

AI will have a significant impact on the nature of employment in the future, necessitating aggressive policy, new practices, and educational reforms.

Policy Frameworks

- **Adapting Labor Laws:** It is imperative to update labor laws in an AI-driven economy to preserve workers' rights and account for new types of employment. This covers laws pertaining to upskilling, retraining, and job relocation.

- **Encouraging Entrepreneurship:** Encouraging entrepreneurship via financial aid, grants, and legislative backing fosters creativity and the creation of jobs in AI-related sectors.

- **Incentives for Adoption of AI:** Offering incentives to companies that use AI ethically can ensure ethical practices while accelerating productivity increases and economic progress.

Modern Curriculum:

- **Educational Revolution:** Computational thinking and AI literacy are included into school curricula to prepare students for professions in AI. This covers data literacy, coding, and moral AI concepts.

- **Lifetime Education:** Encouraging lifelong learning programs guarantees that people can always pick up new skills and adjust to the changing needs of the labor market. This covers apprenticeships, online courses, and career training.

Innovative Work Practices

- **Remote Work and Automation:** Productivity and work-life balance are improved by embracing automation technologies and flexible work schedules. Investments in remote collaboration technologies and digital infrastructure are necessary for this.

- **AI in Making Decisions:** AI decision-making support increases productivity and accuracy across a range of industries, including healthcare and finance, and promotes economic development.

9.2 Technology's Role: Using AI to Advance Human Welfare

Through creative applications, AI offers potential to improve human well-being and solve societal issues.

Medical Advancements

- **Precision Medicine:** AI-powered diagnosis and

individualized treatment regimens enhance patient care quality and healthcare outcomes. This covers the use of AI in patient management software, medication development, and medical imaging.

- **Medicine over the phone:** Increasing access to AI-powered telemedicine platforms improves healthcare delivery, especially in underprivileged areas.

Environmental Sustainability

- **Climate Modeling:** Predictive analytics and AI-powered climate modeling reduce environmental risks and assist guide policy decisions. This involves keeping an eye on attempts to conserve biodiversity, air quality, and deforestation.

- **Green Technology:** AI-driven solutions for resource efficiency, smart grid management, and renewable energy optimization are being developed to promote sustainability and lessen environmental impact.

Social Good Initiatives

- **Disaster Response:** Predictive models driven by artificial intelligence and real-time data analysis enhance efforts to prepare for and respond to disasters. This covers the coordination of humanitarian relief and early warning systems for natural catastrophes.

- **Education Accessibility:** AI-powered learning aids and flexible learning environments facilitate individualized instruction and fair access to high-quality education on a global scale.

9.3 Creating a Sustainable Future: Using AI for Social and Environmental Benefit

AI can be a key tool for accomplishing sustainable development objectives by advancing social justice and environmental preservation.

Resource Management

- **Circular Economy:** AI-driven optimization algorithms enhance waste management and resource allocation strategies, supporting a circular economy model. This covers supply chain sustainability and recycling programs.
- **Analysis of Consumer Behavior:** In order to

promote environmentally friendly consumption habits, sustainable product design and marketing strategies are informed by consumer behavior patterns as analyzed by AI.

Ethical Considerations

- **Fairness and Transparency:** Maintaining moral AI values like accountability, fairness, and transparency guarantees that AI innovations advance society without escalating prejudices or inequities.

- **Privacy Protection:** By putting strong data privacy laws and cybersecurity safeguards in place, users and stakeholders can feel more confident that their personal information in AI applications is protected.

9.4 Promoting Cooperation: Creating a Future That Benefits Everyone

The realization of a future where artificial intelligence is fully utilized calls for broad participation and worldwide cooperation.

Global Collaboration

- **Exchange of Knowledge:** Accelerating technical developments and promoting creativity are achieved through fostering international collaboration in AI research and development. This covers cooperative projects, gatherings, and collaborations in research.

- **Harmonization of Policies:** The creation of international norms and moral principles for the application of AI guarantees uniformity and cross-border compatibility, promoting the responsible adoption of AI globally.

Innovation Ecosystems

- **Public-Private Partnerships:** Public-private collaborations that foster an environment that is helpful to AI companies and entrepreneurs promote economic growth and job creation. This covers venture capital investments as well as incubators and accelerators.

- **Enterprise Liability:** Businesses are guaranteed to give ethical considerations, social effect, and sustainability top priority in their operations when corporate responsibility is encouraged in AI development and deployment.

Community Engagement

- **Stakeholder Involvement:** Including a range of stakeholders in AI governance processes, including as academic institutions, local communities, and civil society organizations, fosters inclusion and democratic decision-making.

- **Public Awareness:** Dispelling myths and worries around artificial intelligence (AI) while increasing public knowledge of AI technology, their advantages, and any hazards.

Thoughtful decisions on collaboration, innovation, education, and policy will determine the direction of AI in the future. We can create a future in which artificial intelligence (AI) advances society and raises everyone's standard of living by adopting moral behavior, using technology for good, encouraging sustainability, and supporting inclusive growth. This calls for proactive leadership, international collaboration, and a dedication to creating a future that benefits all.

CHAPTER 10

The New Work Era

The nature of work is rapidly evolving in the era of artificial intelligence (AI), bringing with it both new opportunities and challenges. Here examines the importance of lifelong learning, the accessibility of AI technology, the range of future employment opportunities, and concludes with some encouraging ideas on embracing change.

10.1 Developing a Lifelong Learning Perspective: Adjusting to Constant Change

Adopting a lifelong learning mentality is essential for remaining relevant and succeeding in an AI-driven future as technology advances.

Continuous Skill Development

- **Adapting to Change:** People must constantly update their knowledge and skills since they may find that what they need now won't be sufficient tomorrow.

- **Upskilling and Reskilling:** It is imperative to make investments in educational opportunities and training programs that provide people with digital fluency, data analysis abilities, and AI literacy.

- **Professional Development:** Participating in lifelong learning activities promotes career progression and adaptability in changing employment markets. Examples of these initiatives include online courses, workshops, and mentorship programs.

Navigating professional Transitions

- **Career Mobility:** Accepting professional shifts and seizing fresh chances made possible by AI technology fosters resilience and personal development in the face of shifting economic conditions.

- **Spirit of Entrepreneurship:** Developing an entrepreneurial attitude promotes creativity, risk-taking, and innovation while using AI to launch new businesses and disrupt existing markets.

10.2 Democratizing AI Tools: The Emergence of the Citizen Scientist

The democratization of AI enables people from a variety of backgrounds to engage in and make contributions to innovation, scientific inquiry, and problem-solving.

Available AI Technologies

- **Open-Source Platforms:** Making use of open-source AI tools and platforms democratizes access to cutting-edge technologies and fosters creativity and cooperation across international communities.

- **Crowdsourced Data Analysis:** Including citizen scientists in data gathering, analysis, and interpretation increases the capacity for research and hastens the advancement of science across a range of fields.

- **Involvement in the Community:** Encouraging diverse viewpoints and inclusive engagement in AI development guarantees that AI solutions successfully solve social issues.

Ethical Considerations

- **Transparency and Trust:** Ensuring ethical rules prevent misuse or bias in AI applications, as well as maintaining transparency in AI development processes.

- **Data Privacy:** Encouraging involvement in citizen science projects and fostering trust are two benefits of safeguarding user privacy and data security in AI-driven projects.

10.3 A World of Possibilities for the Future of Work

Flexibility, creativity, and human-AI collaboration will define the nature of employment in the future, opening up a wide range of opportunities for different businesses.

Adaptable Work Environments

- **Remote Work:** Incorporating AI-supported remote work choices improves work-life balance and productivity for workers globally.

- **Gig Economy:** By facilitating freelancing and gig opportunities through digital platforms and marketplaces driven by artificial intelligence, independent workers can gain financial empowerment and flexibility.

AI-Augmented Roles

- **Human-AI Collaboration:** Using AI systems in tandem to improve efficiency across a range of industries, such as manufacturing, healthcare, and finance, by automating repetitive tasks and augmenting decision-making.

- **New employment Roles:** To meet changing market needs and technology demands, new employment roles are emerging, such as data stewards, virtual reality designers, and AI ethicists.

10.4 A Final Thought: Optimistically Accepting Change

To fully realize AI's promise, we must negotiate its revolutionary impact on the future of work and society. Proactive adaptation and an optimistic outlook on change are essential.

Embracing Innovation

- **Cultural Shift:** Fostering an innovative, resilient,

and always improving culture makes it easier to respond adaptably to social shifts and technological disruptions.

- **Global Collaboration:** Cooperation amongst nations, sectors, and academic fields fosters knowledge exchange, a diversity of viewpoints, and group problem-solving.

Ethical Leadership

- **Responsibility and Accountability:** Maintaining moral principles, encouraging inclusivity and diversity, and giving human-centered values first priority guarantee that the benefits of AI developments are distributed fairly among all members of society.

- **Empowering Individuals:** Giving people the tools they need to succeed in the AI era and help create a bright future is possible through education, technological access, and skill-development opportunities.

In conclusion, there are chances for creativity, teamwork, and personal development in the new AI-driven workplace future. People and society can manage the intricacies of the AI revolution and build an inclusive, sustainable, and successful future for all by embracing lifelong learning, democratizing AI tools, investigating a variety of employment options, and approaching change with positivity.

ABOUT THE AUTHOR

 Author and thought leader in the IT field Taylor Royce is well known. He has a two-decade career and is an expert at tech trend analysis and forecasting, which enables a wide audience to understand complicated concepts.

Royce's considerable involvement in the IT industry stemmed from his passion with technology, which he developed during his computer science studies. He has extensive knowledge of the industry because of his experience in both software development and strategic consulting.

Known for his research and lucidity, he has written multiple best-selling books and contributed to esteemed tech periodicals. Translations of Royce's books throughout the world demonstrate his impact.

Royce is a well-known authority on emerging technologies and their effects on society, frequently requested as a speaker at international conferences and as a guest on tech podcasts. He promotes the development of ethical technology, emphasizing problems like data privacy and the digital divide.

In addition, with a focus on sustainable industry growth, Royce mentors upcoming tech experts and supports IT education projects. Taylor Royce is well known for his ability to combine analytical thinking with technical know-how. He sees a time when technology will ethically benefit humanity.

www.ingramcontent.com/pod-product-compliance
Lightning Source LLC
LaVergne TN
LVHW051706050326
832903LV00032B/4031